Color With Your Besties
Sherri Baldy
Coloring Books

About The Artist

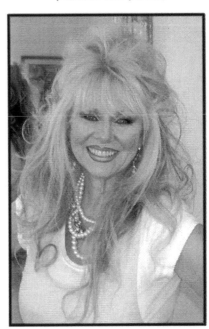

Sherri Baldy is known for her trademark Big Eyed art for over 20 plus years around the world. She is a multi media artist that is licensed on a wide range of products. Sherri lives in Riverside, Calif. with her husband on their farm (Urban Farm Diva Farms) She has two sons Kyler & Josh & two daughter Courtney & Brittany.

When she is not painting, drawing and creating craft products for the craft industry, she spends her time in the gardens at the farm and in her "Barn Studio" that is open to the public by appointment.
Sherri Baldy is now offering her Big Eyed My-Bestie artwork in coloring books.
These fun coloring books come with 2 copies of each image for you to color, or better yet, have a Bestie party and color with one of your Besties Pals or keep them all to yourself :-)
Most of all have FUN, Color, Relax and Enjoy!

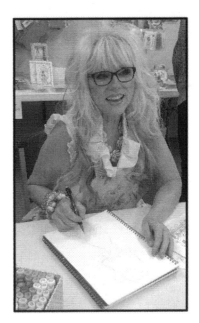

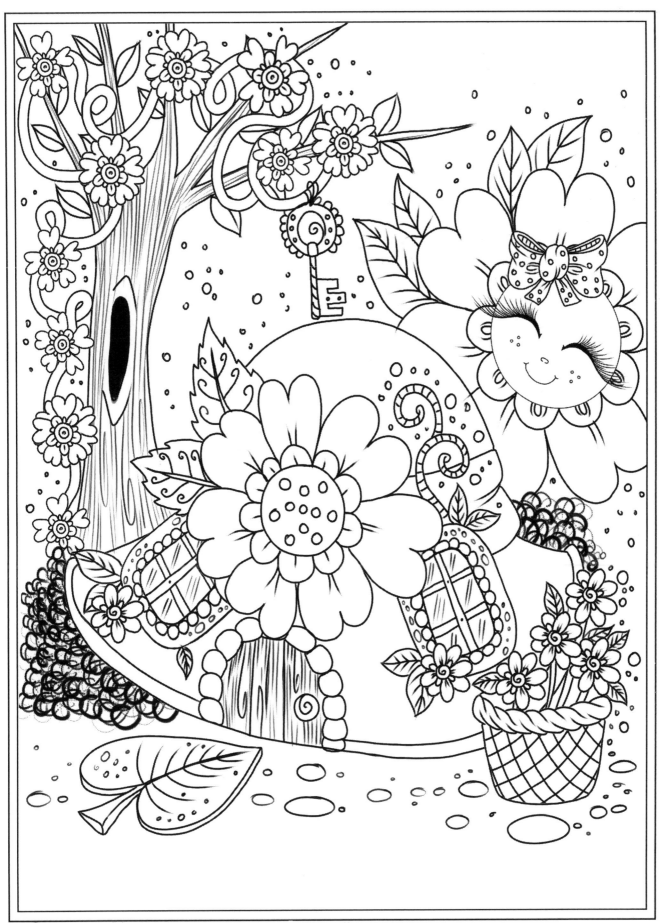

© Sherri Baldy My-Besties Flower Town Hat-ville

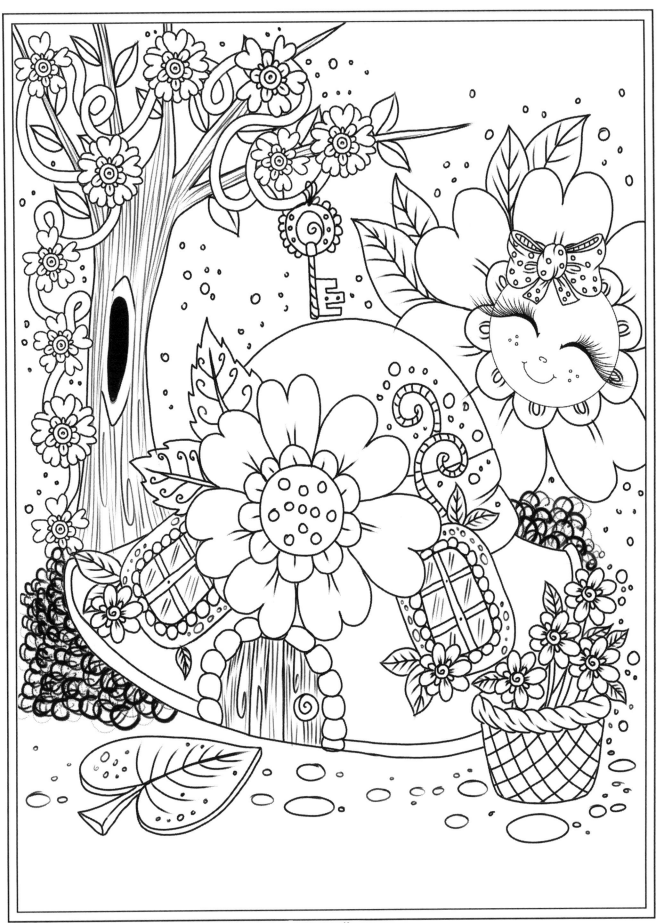

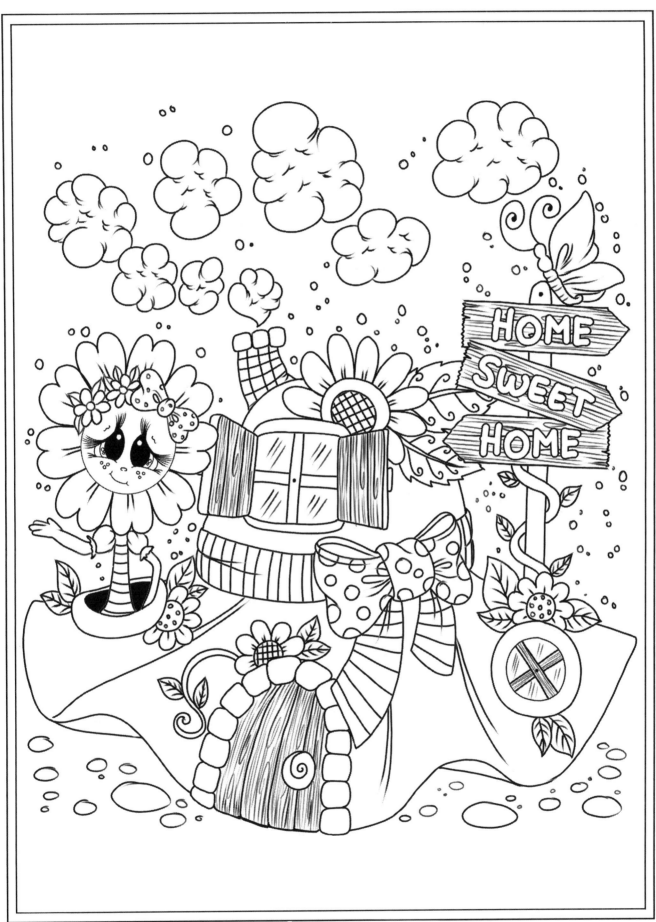

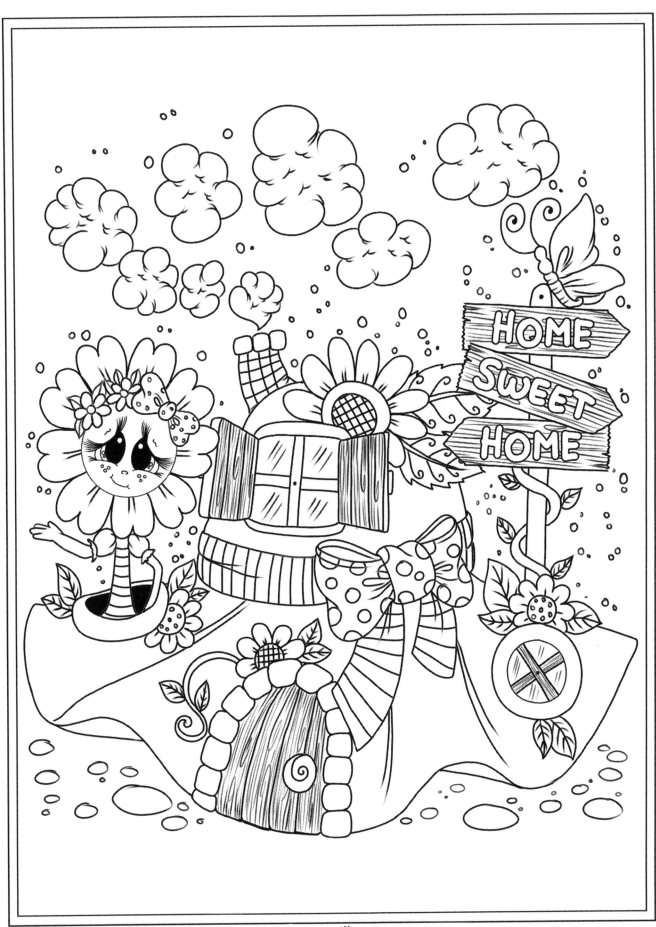

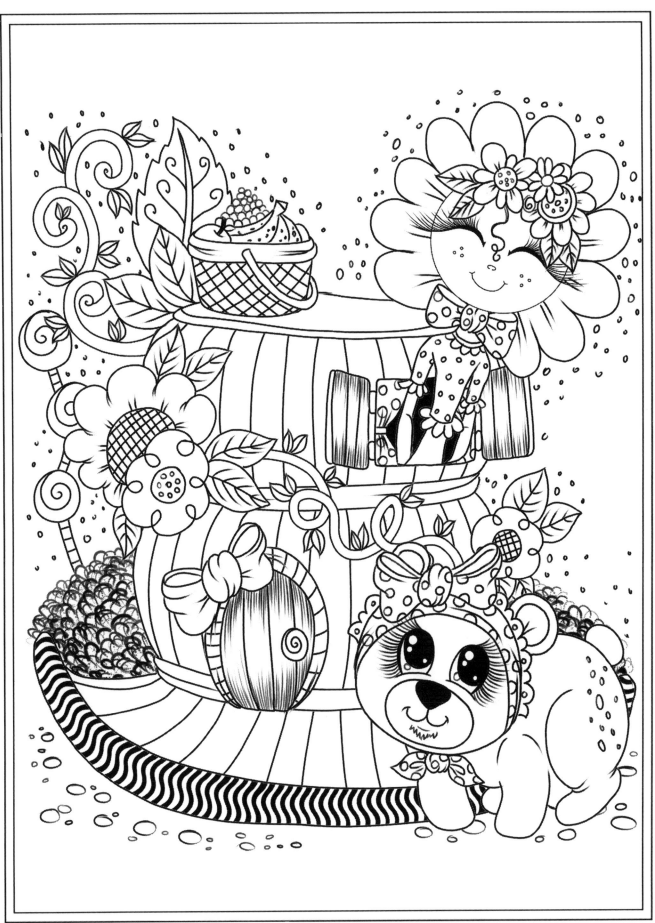

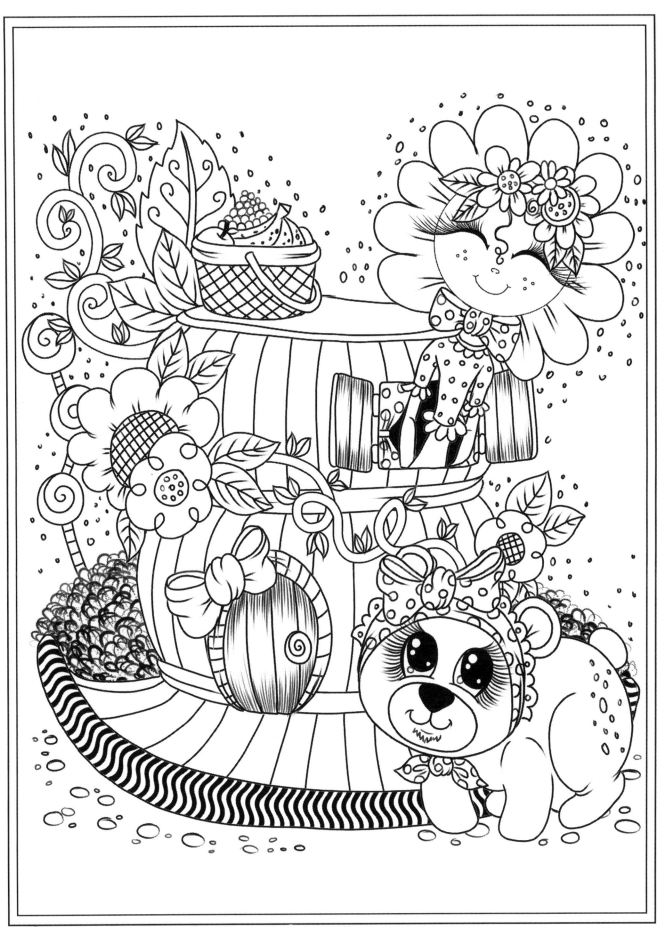

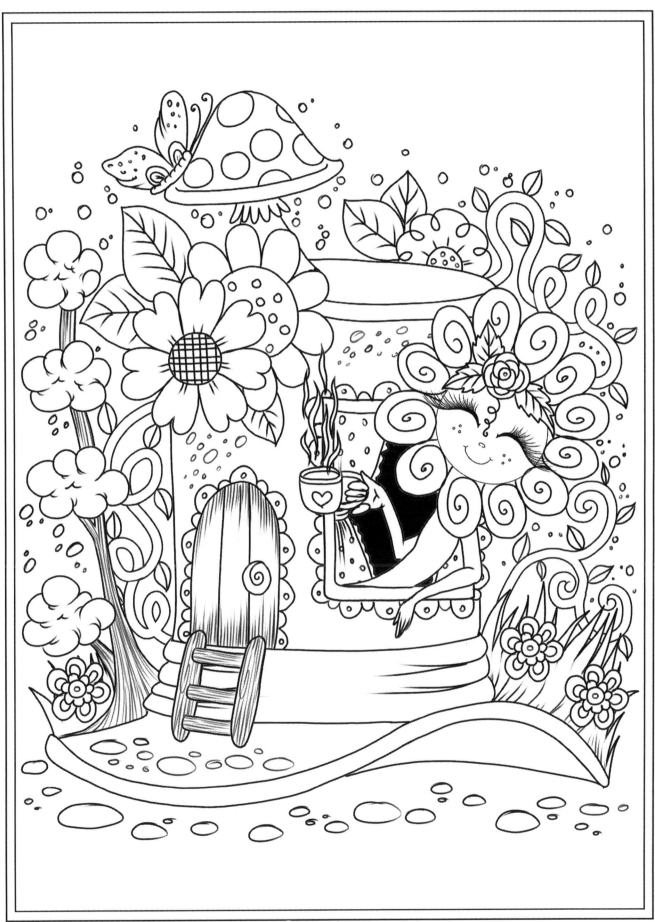

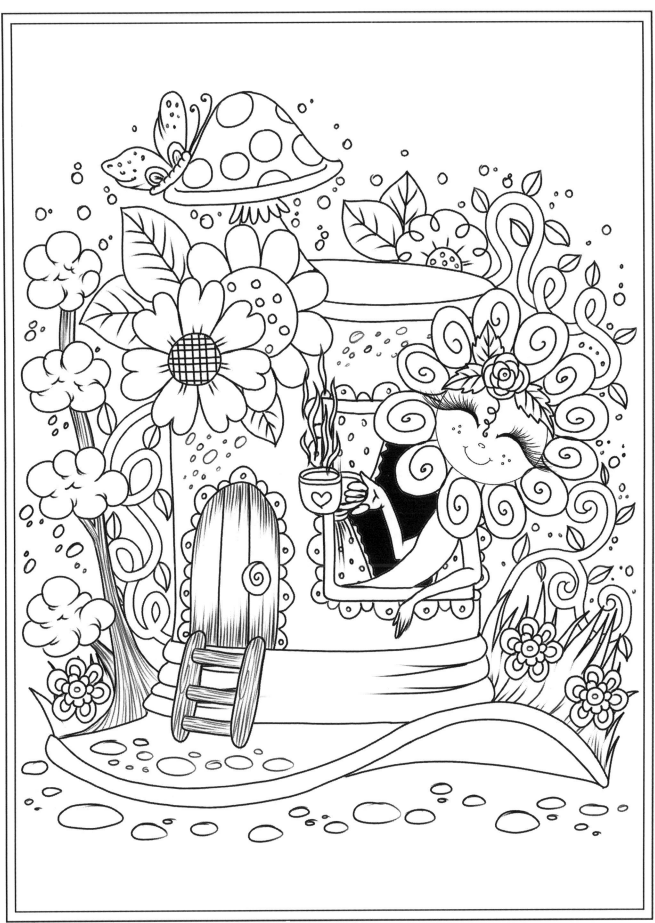

© Sherri Baldy My-Besties Flower Town Hat-ville

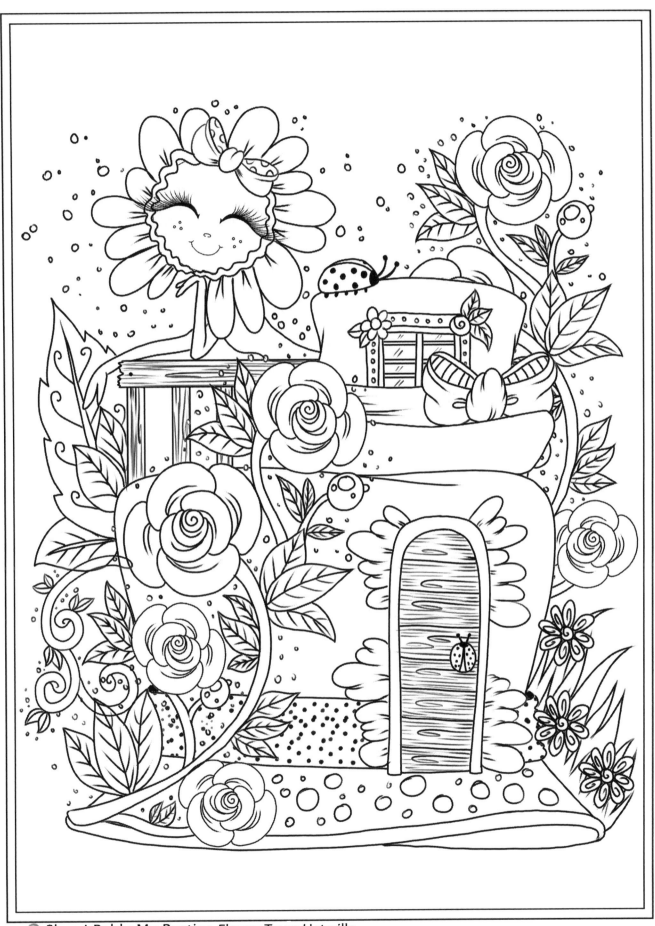

© Sherri Baldy My-Besties Flower Town Hat-ville

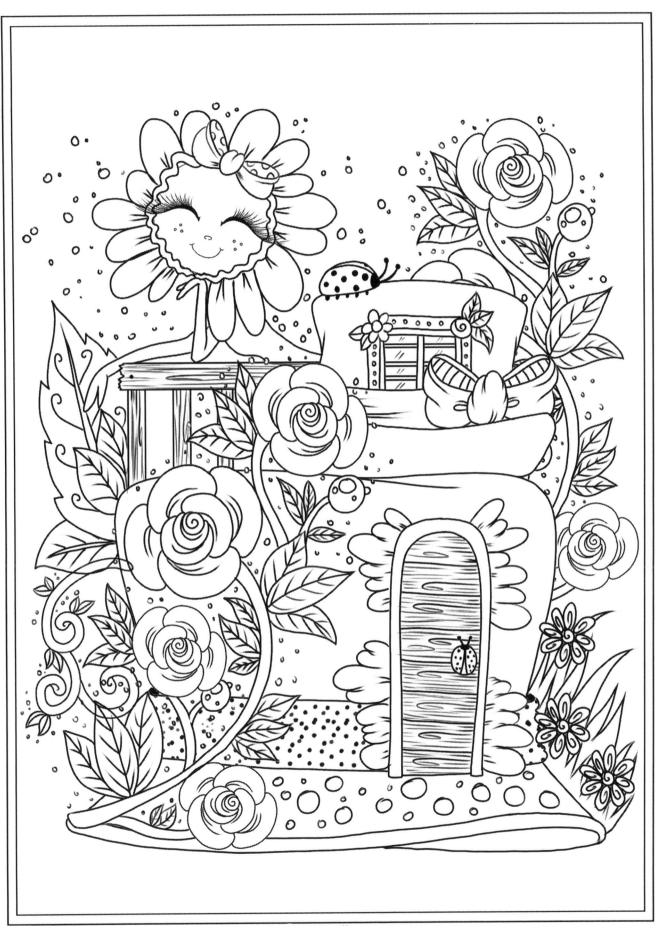

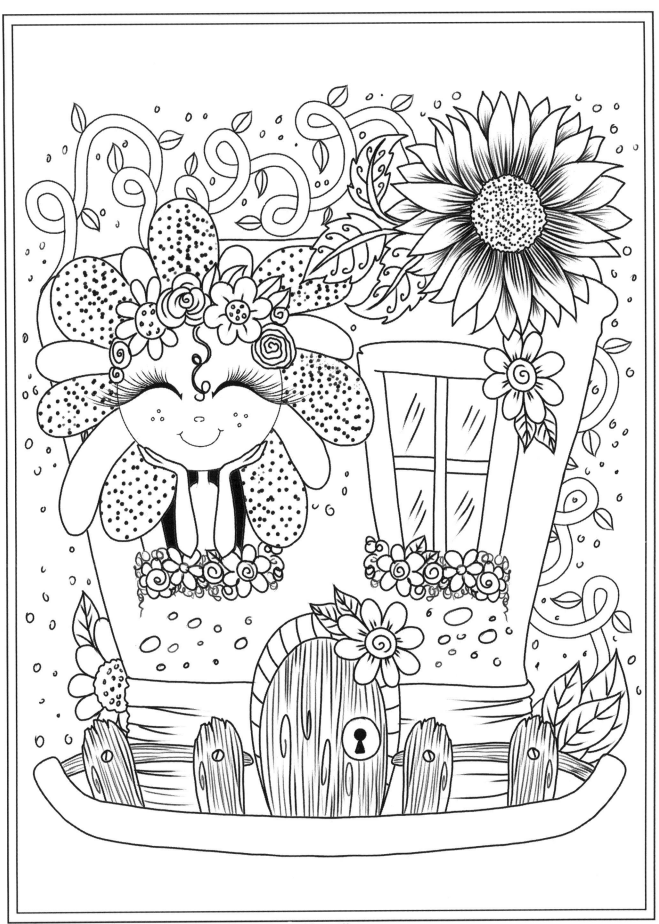

© Sherri Baldy My-Besties Flower Town Hat-ville

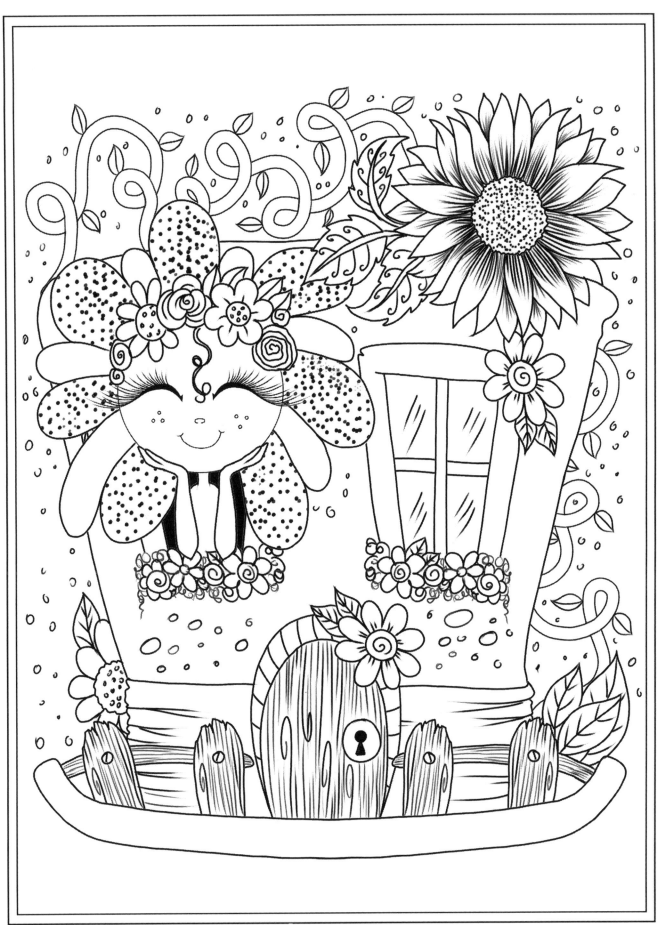

© Sherri Baldy My-Besties Flower Town Hat-ville

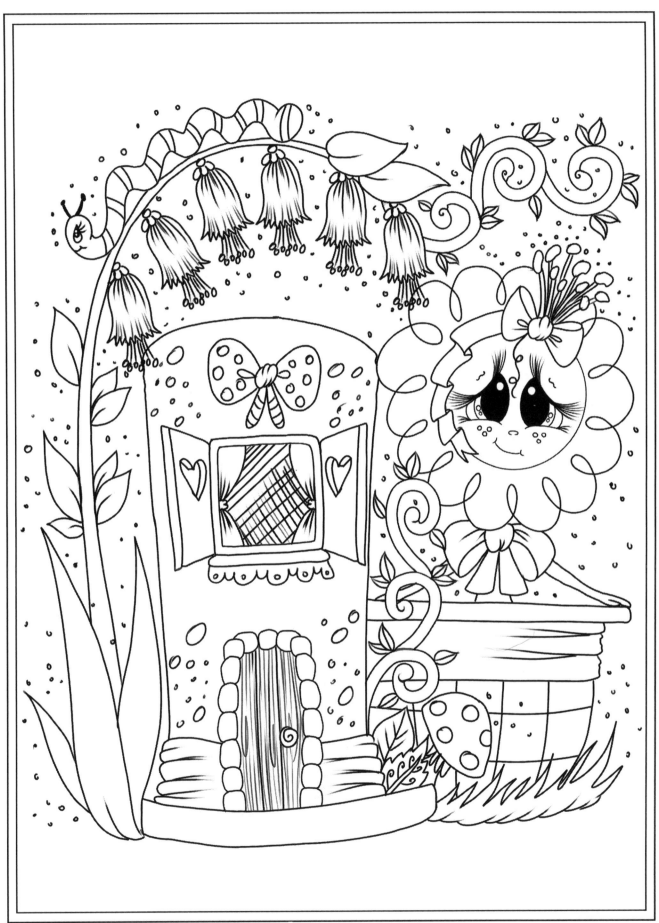

© Sherri Baldy My-Besties Flower Town Hat-ville

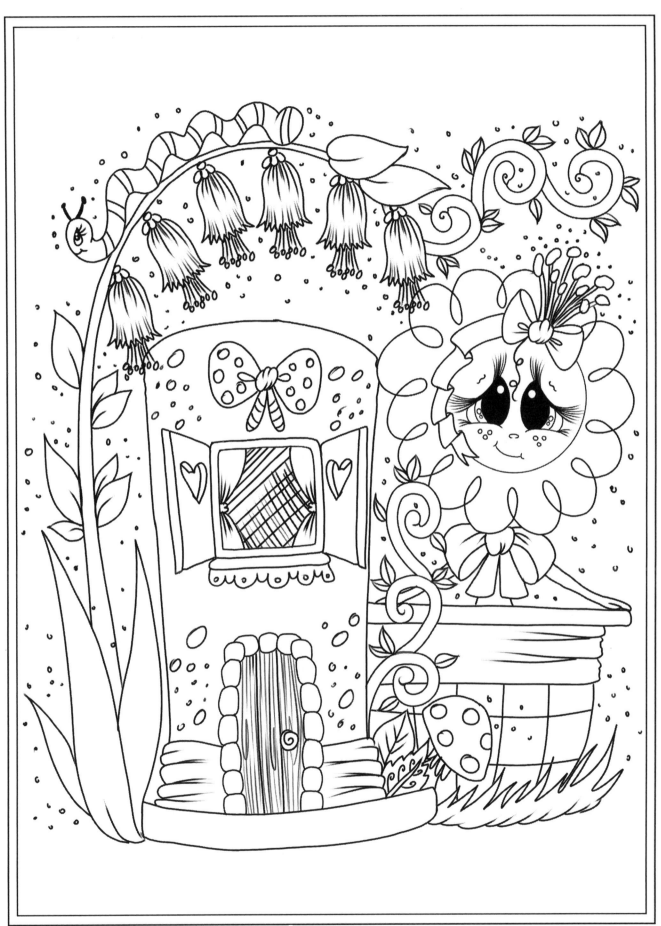

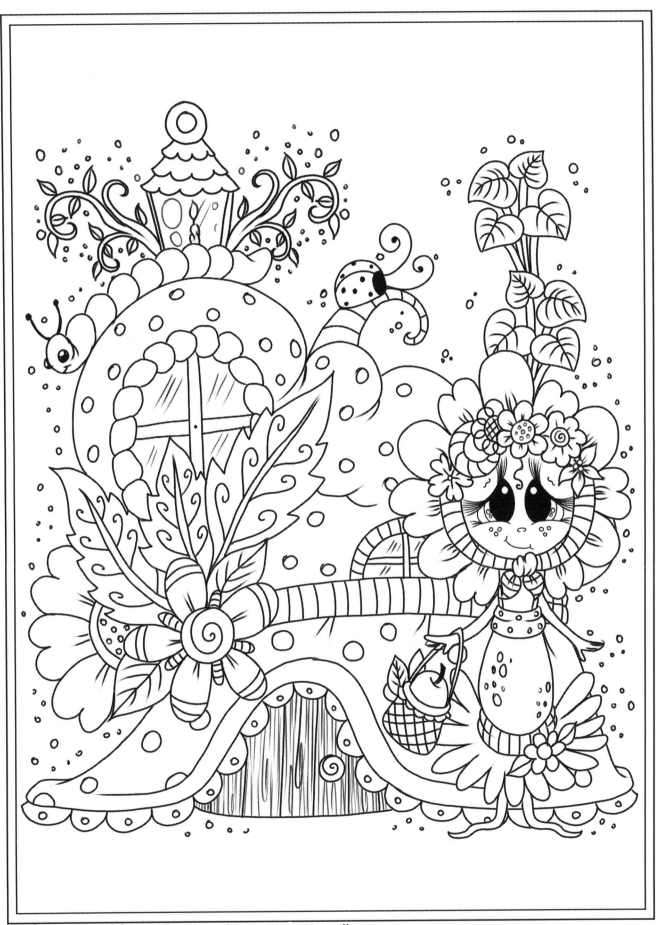

© Sherri Baldy My-Besties Flower Town Hat-ville

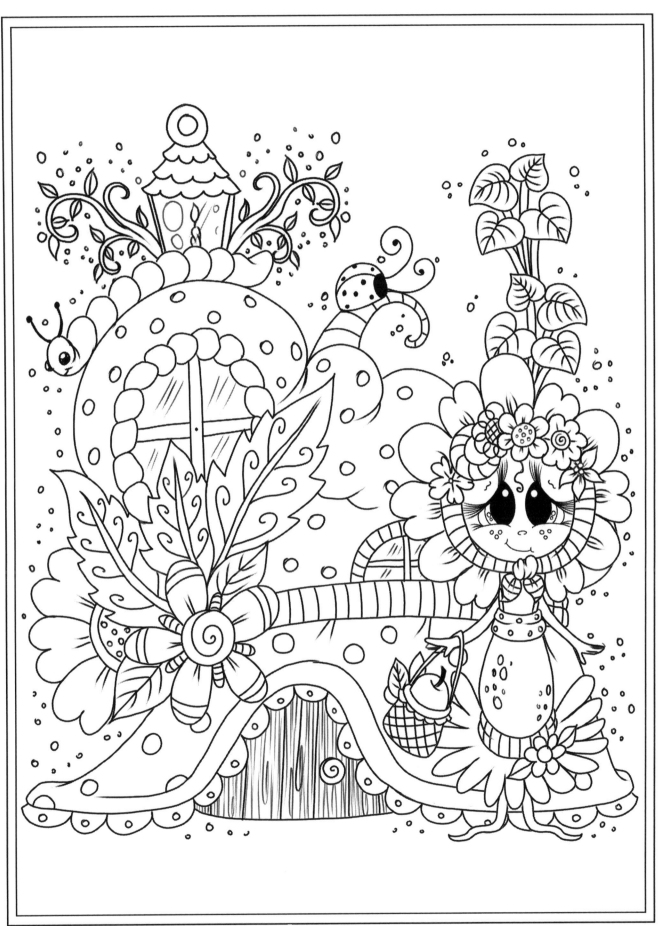

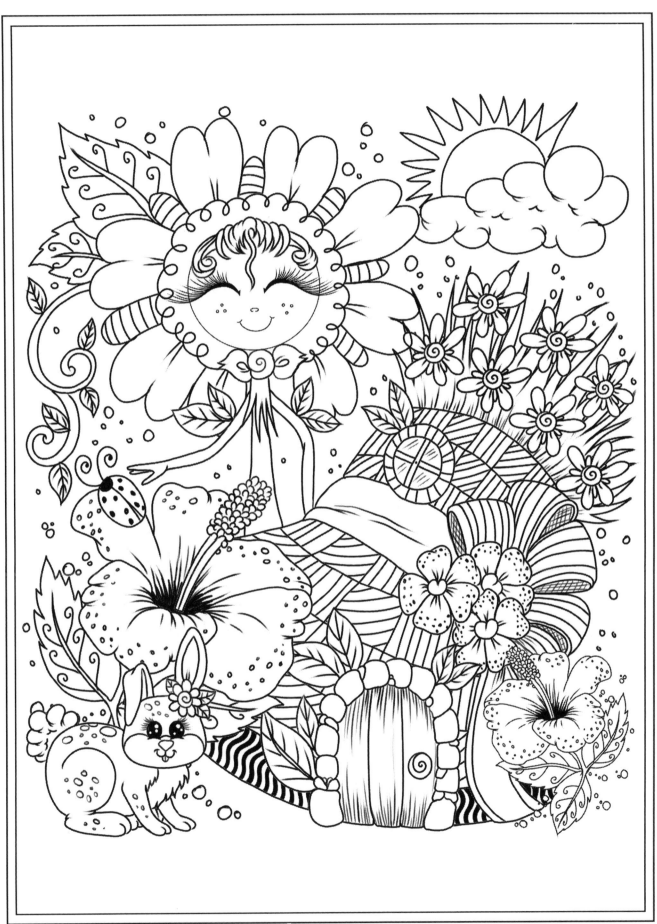

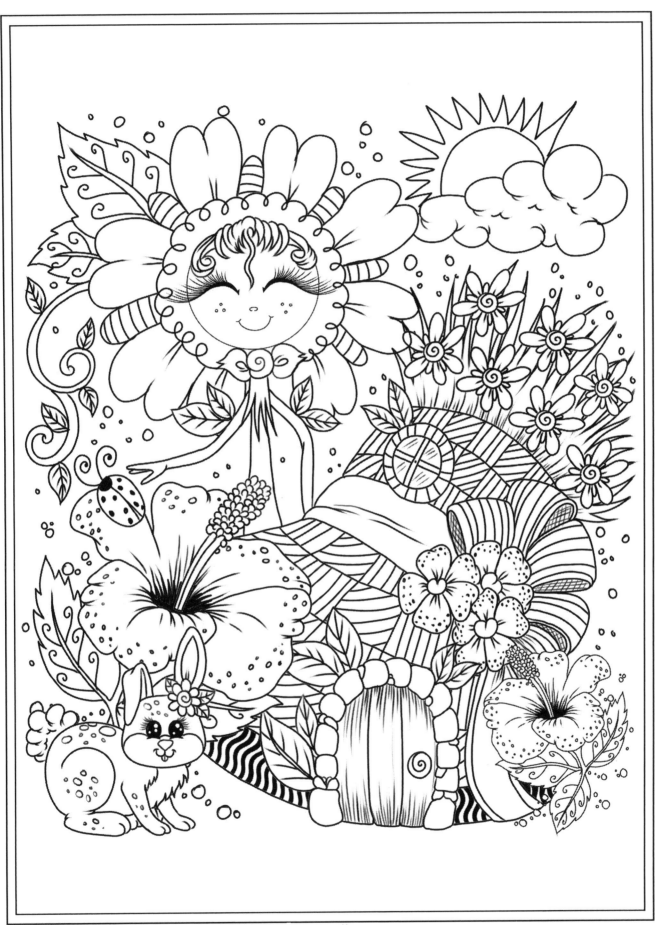

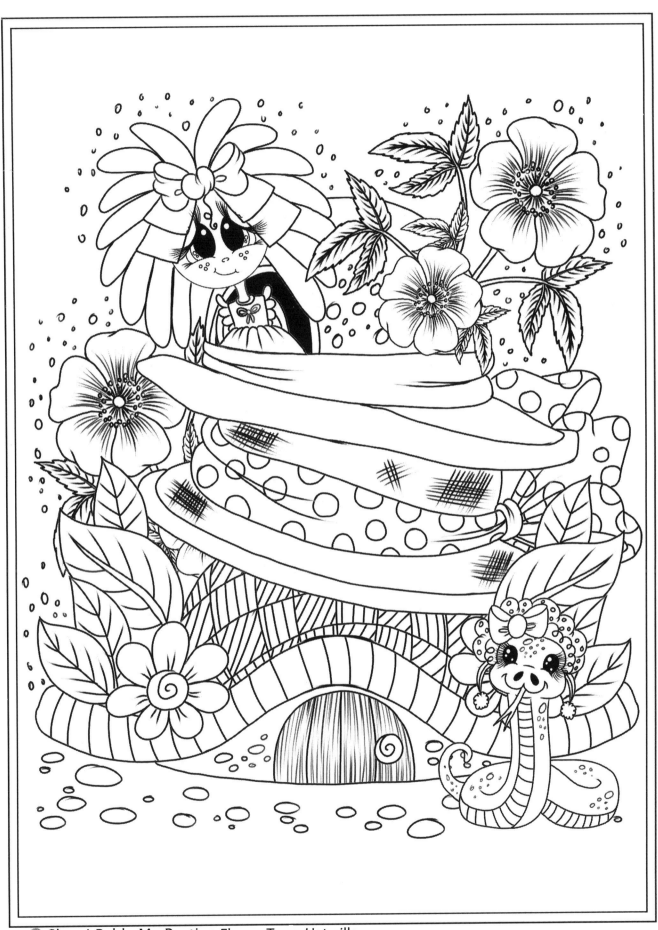

© Sherri Baldy My-Besties Flower Town Hat-ville

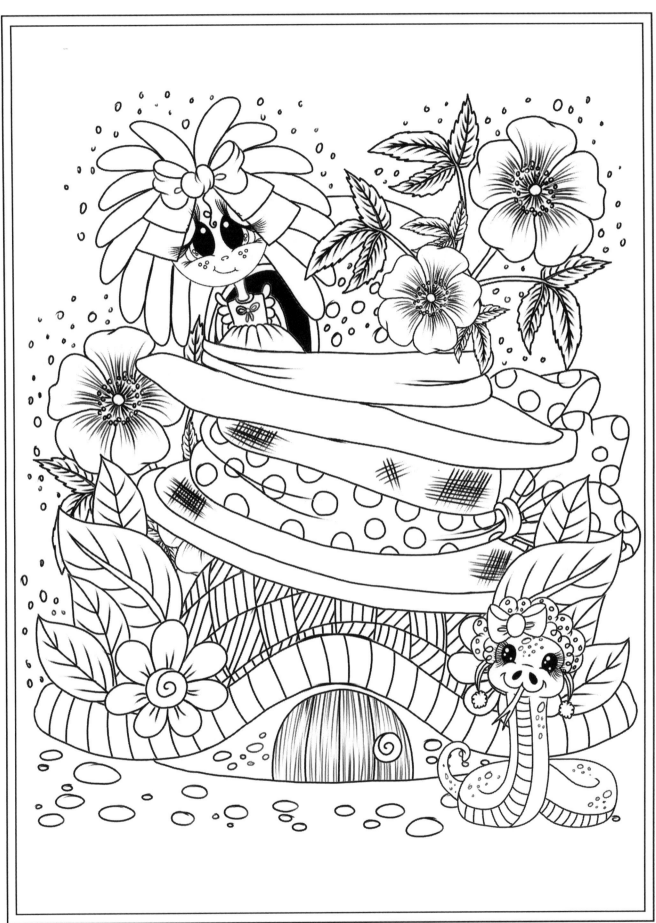

© Sherri Baldy My-Besties Flower Town Hat-ville

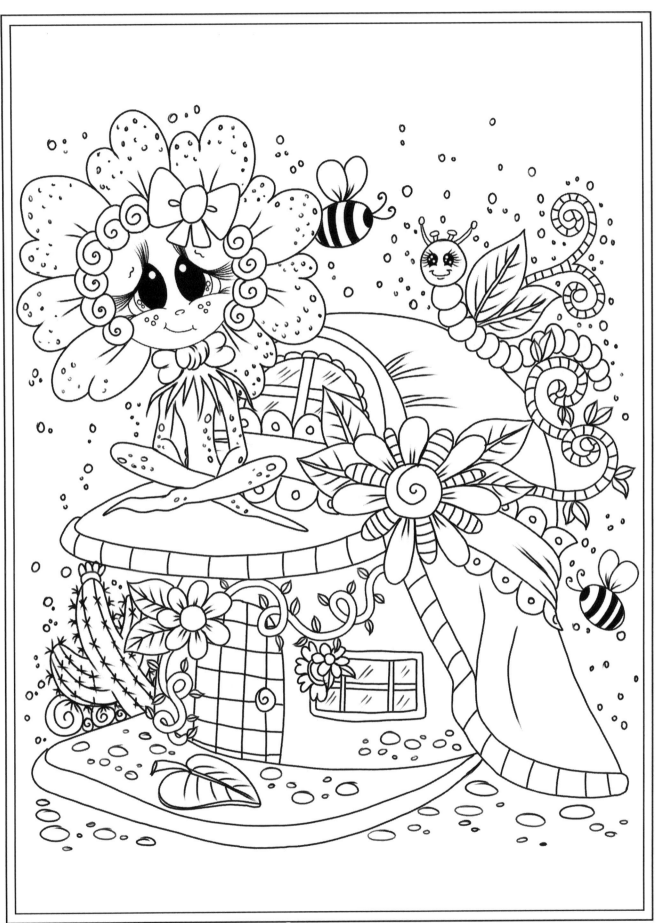

© Sherri Baldy My-Besties Flower Town Hat-ville

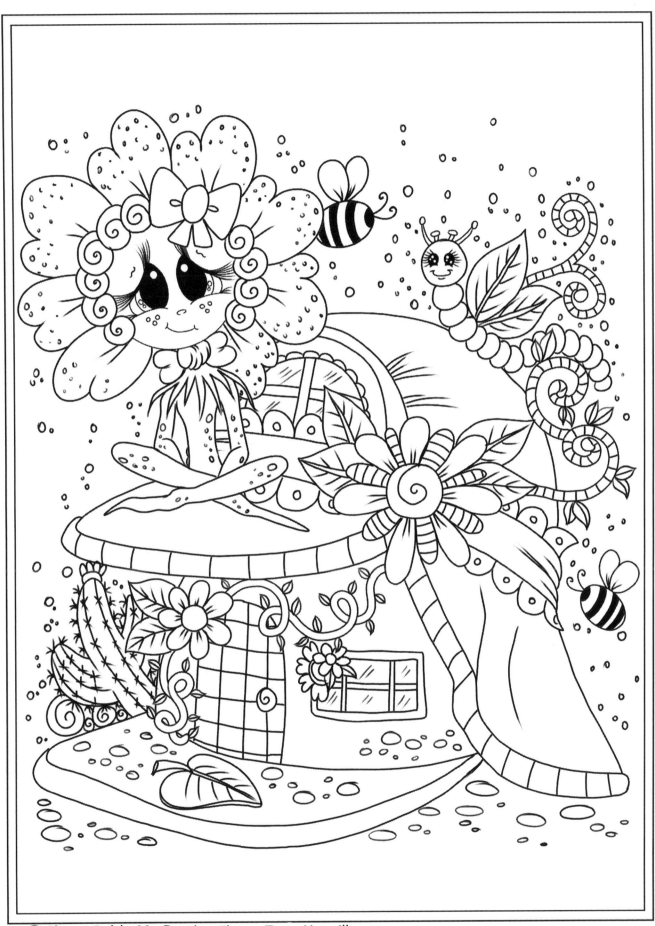

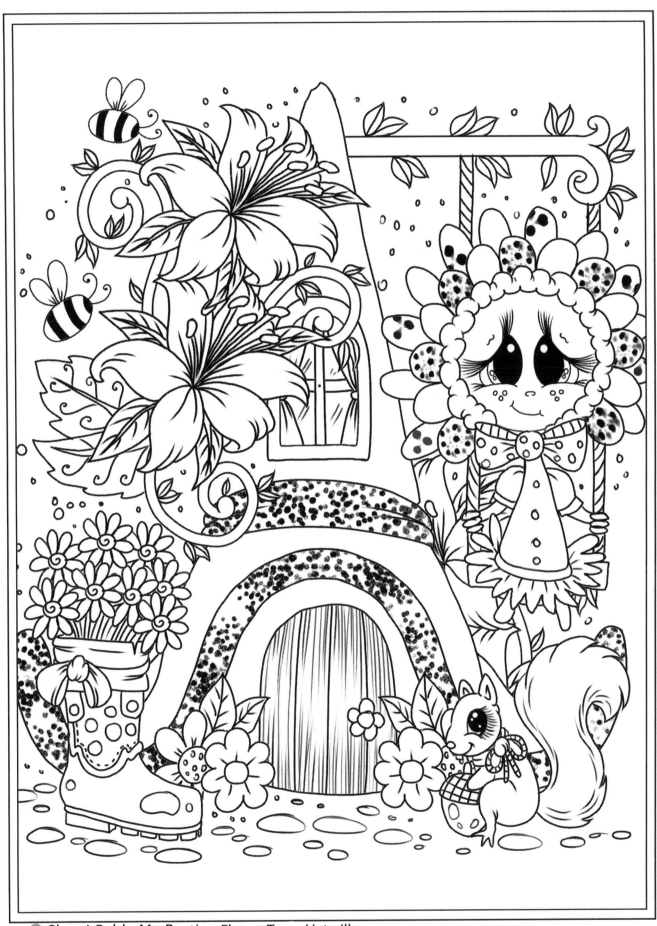

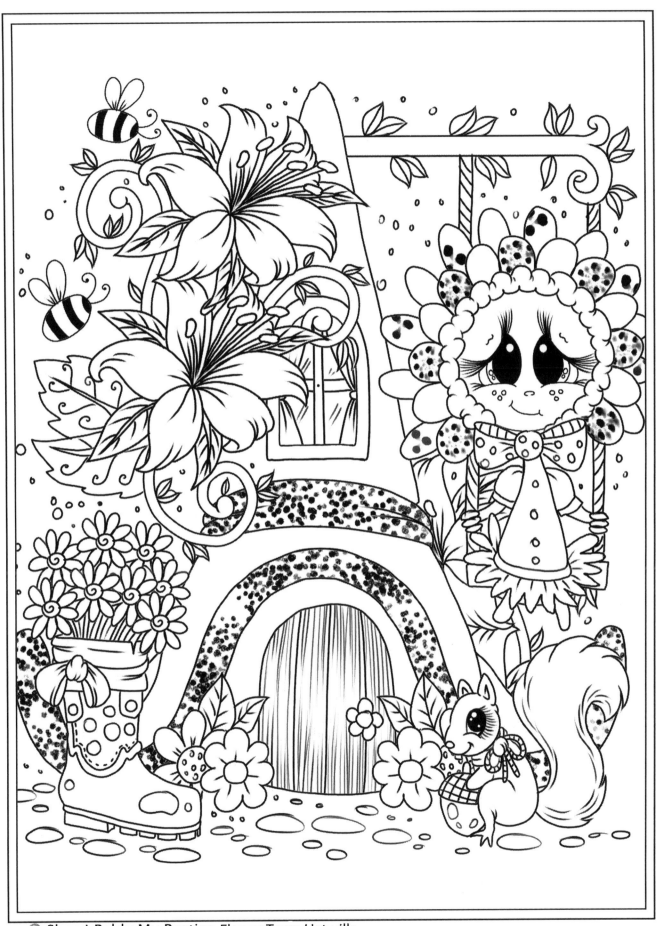

© Sherri Baldy My-Besties Flower Town Hat-ville

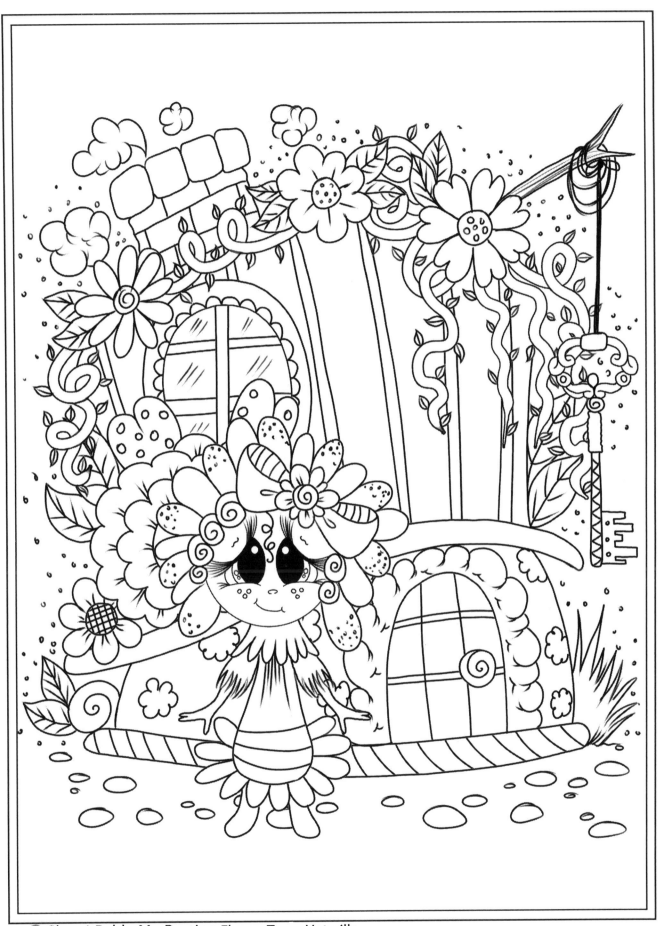

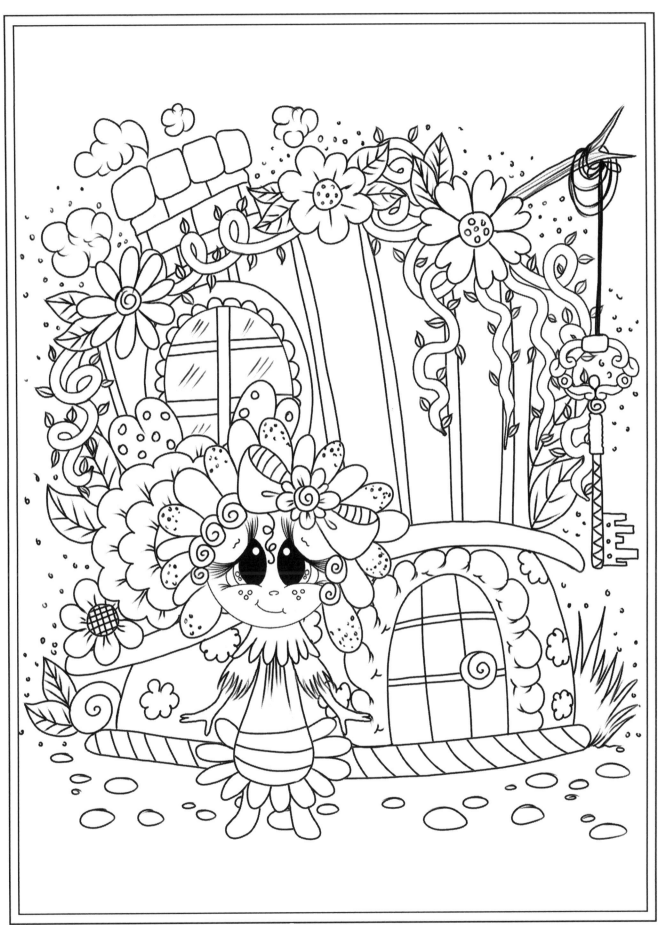

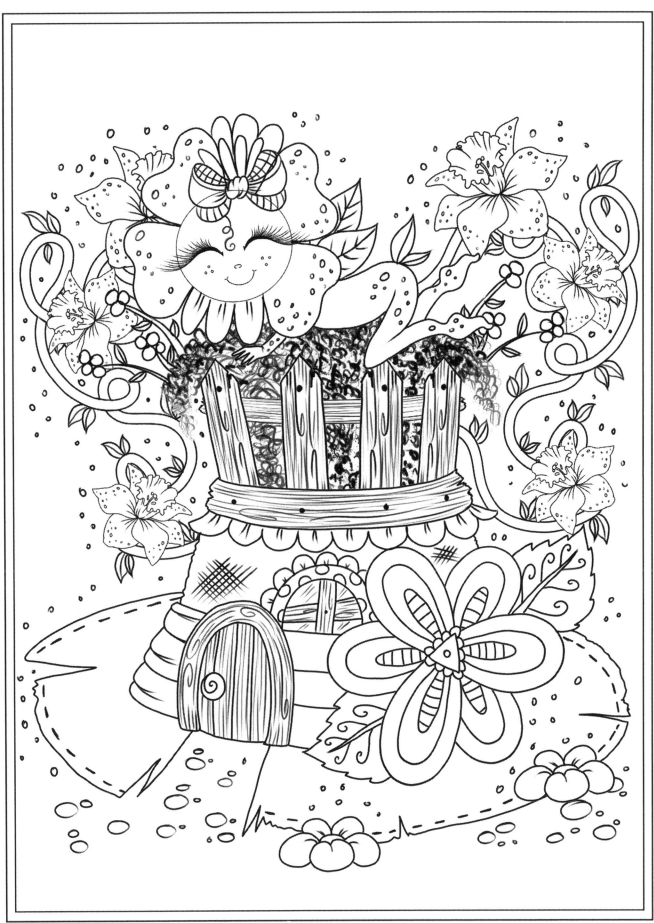

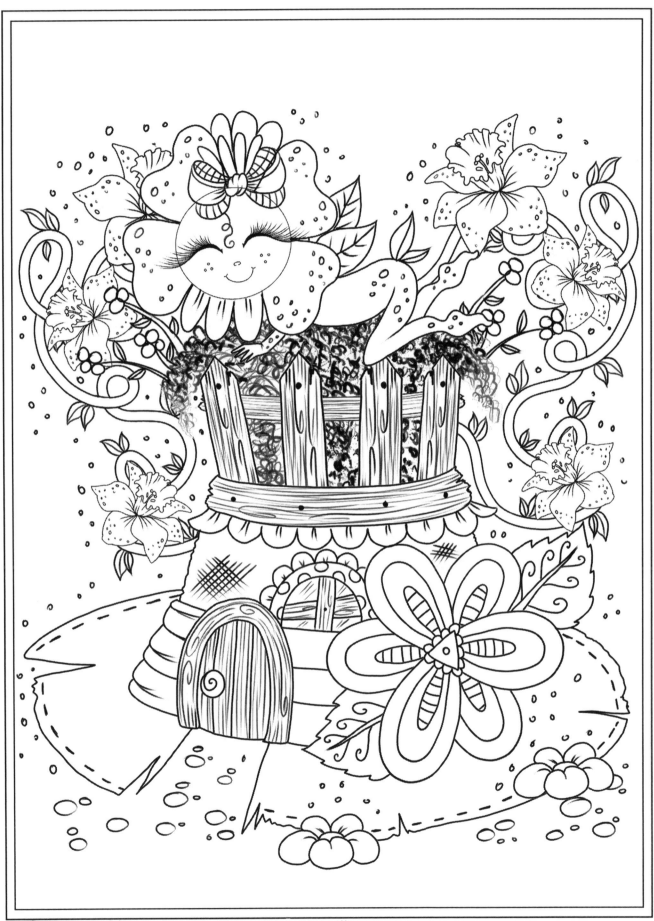

© Sherri Baldy My-Besties Flower Town Hat-ville

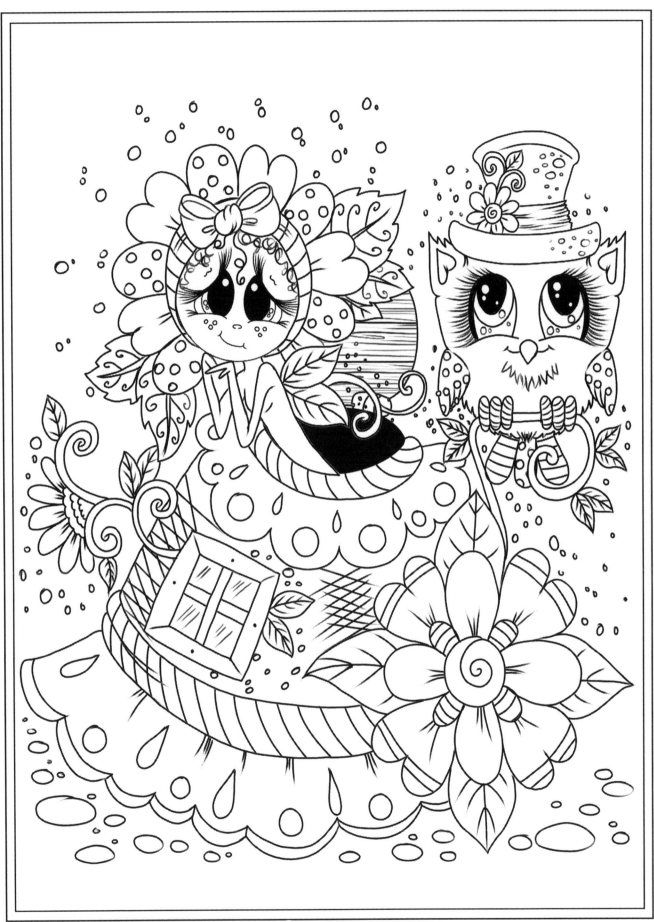

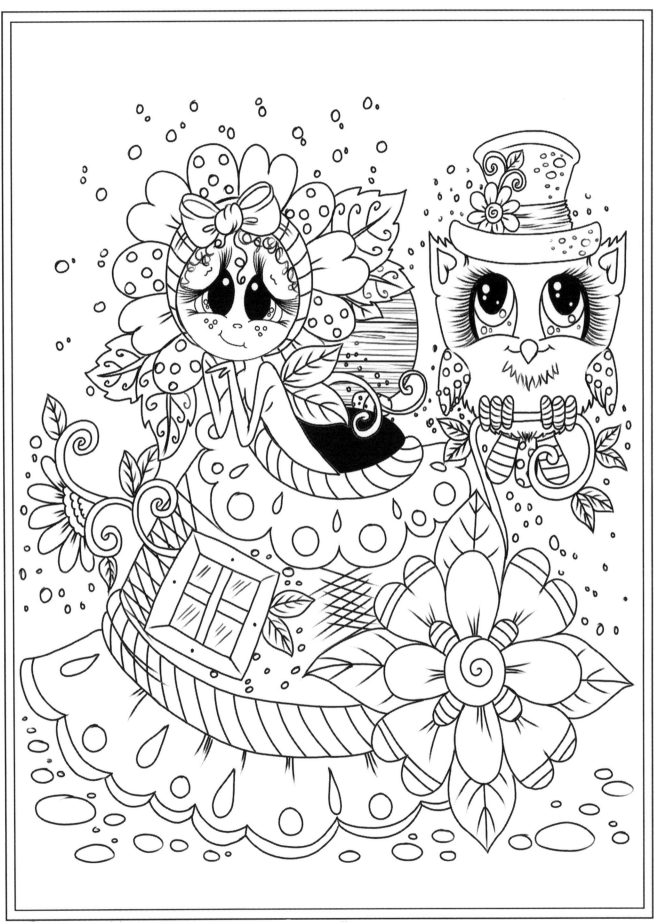

© Sherri Baldy My-Besties Flower Town Hat-ville

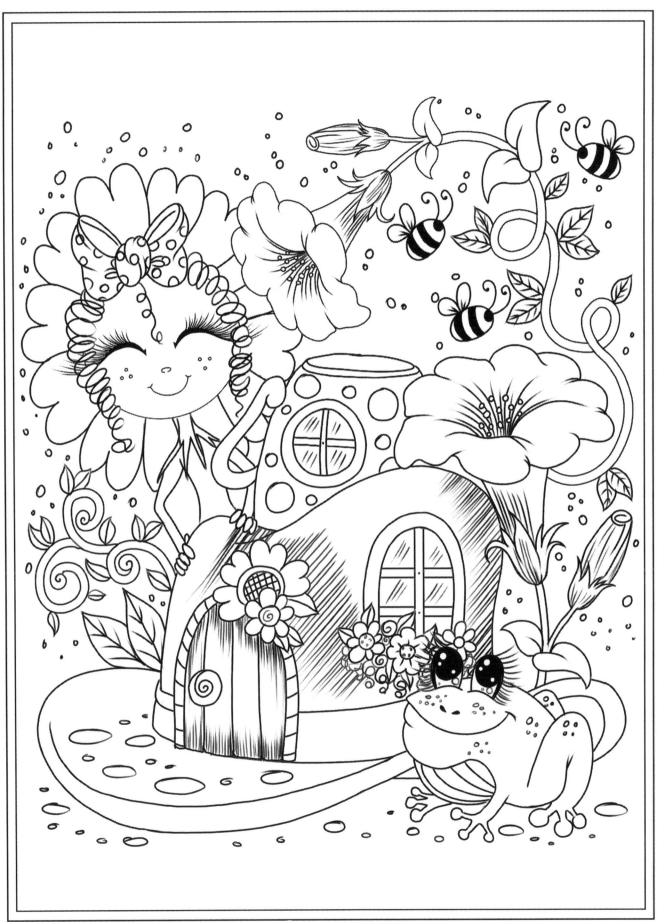

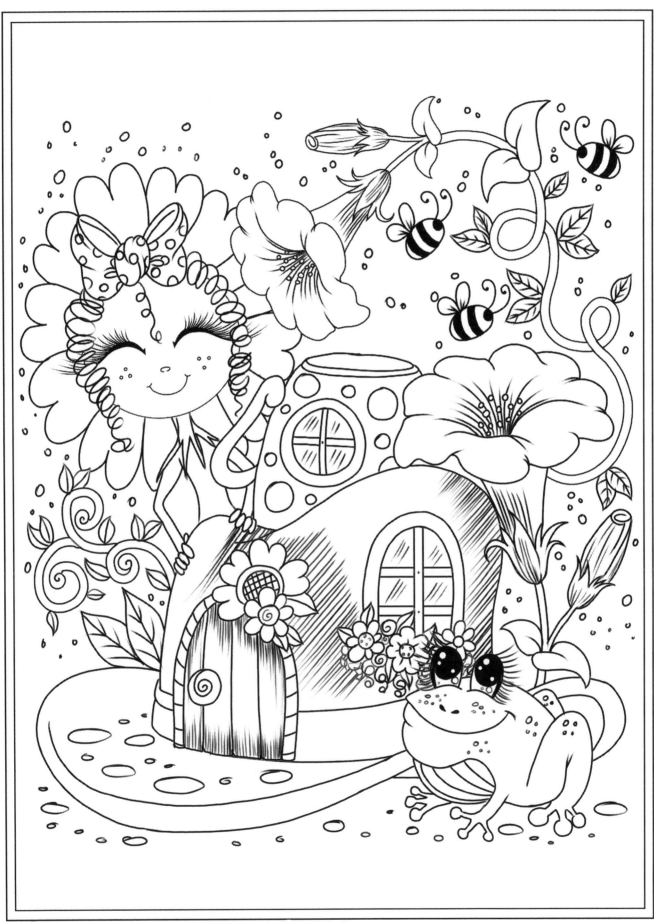

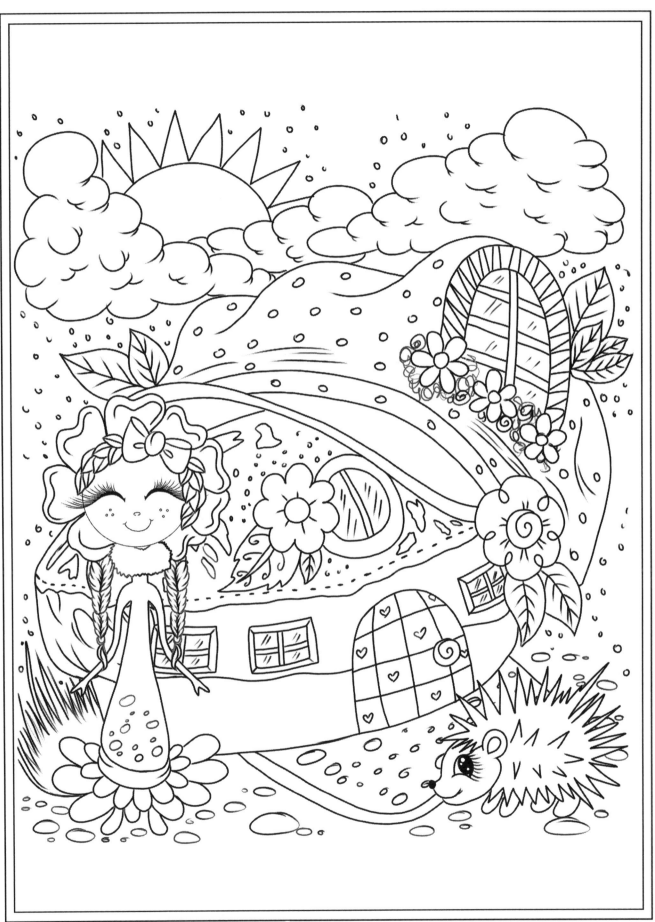

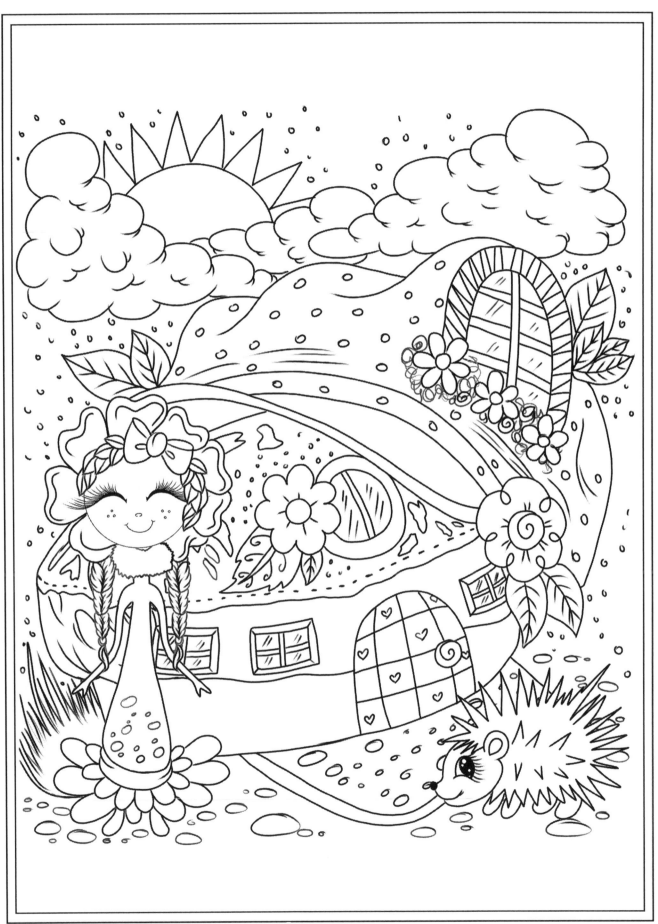

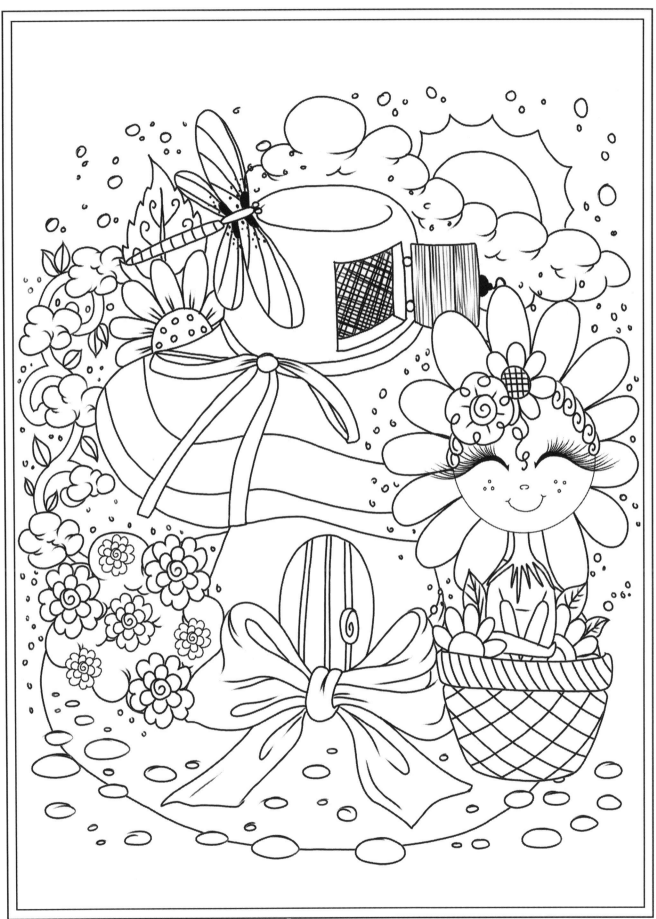

© Sherri Baldy My-Besties Flower Town Hat-ville

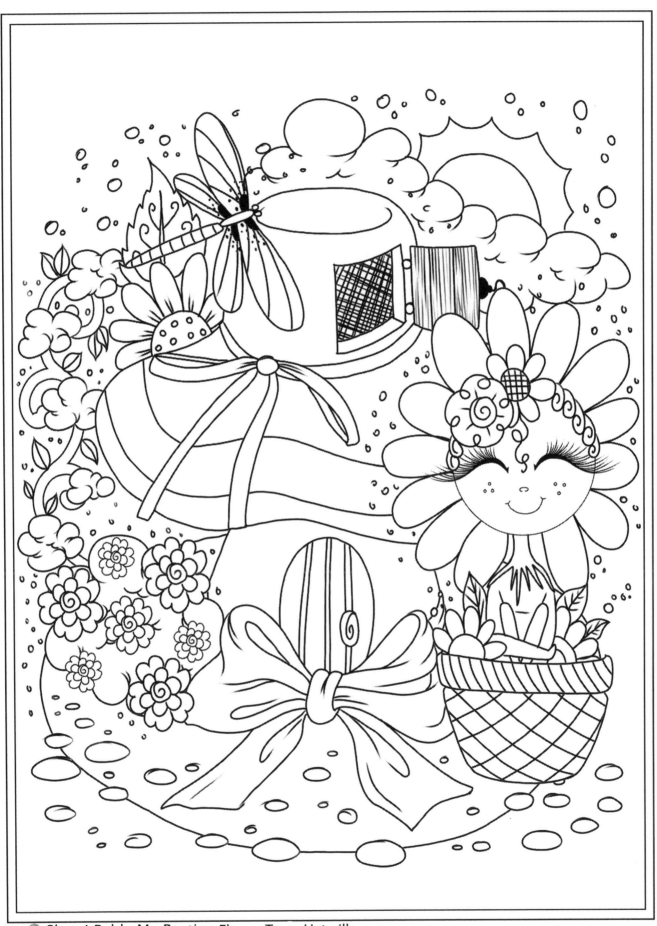

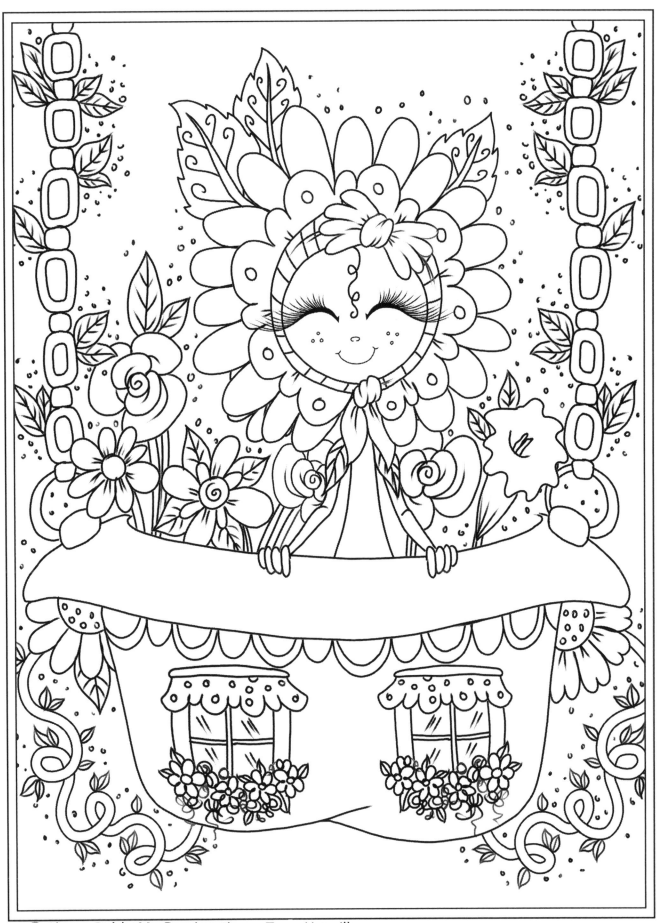

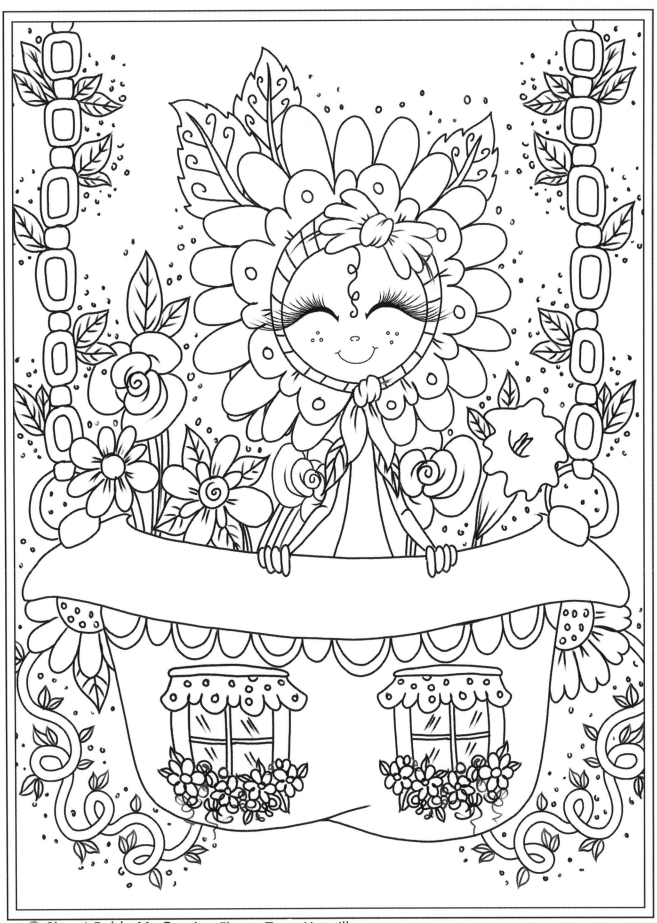

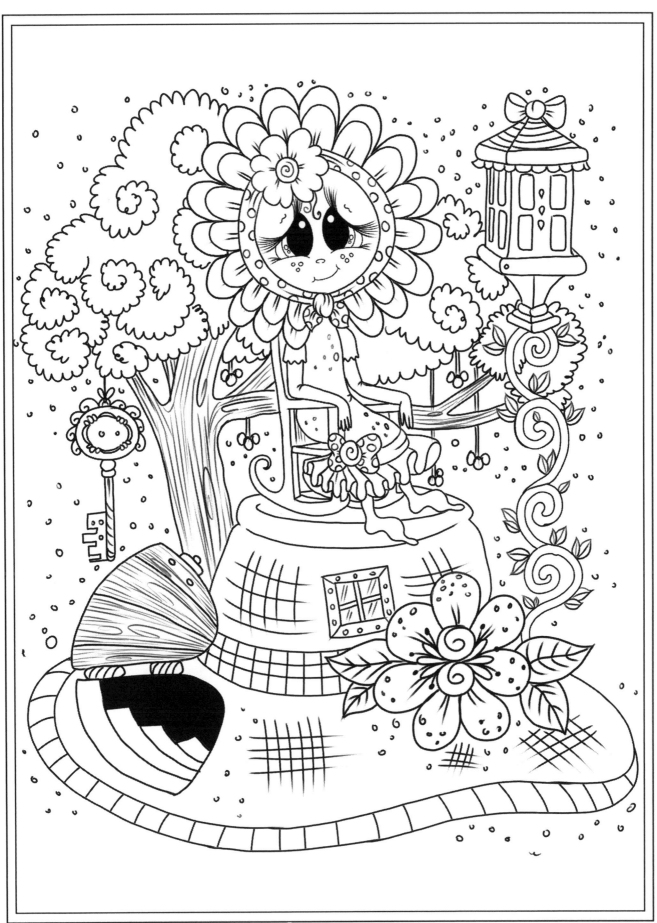

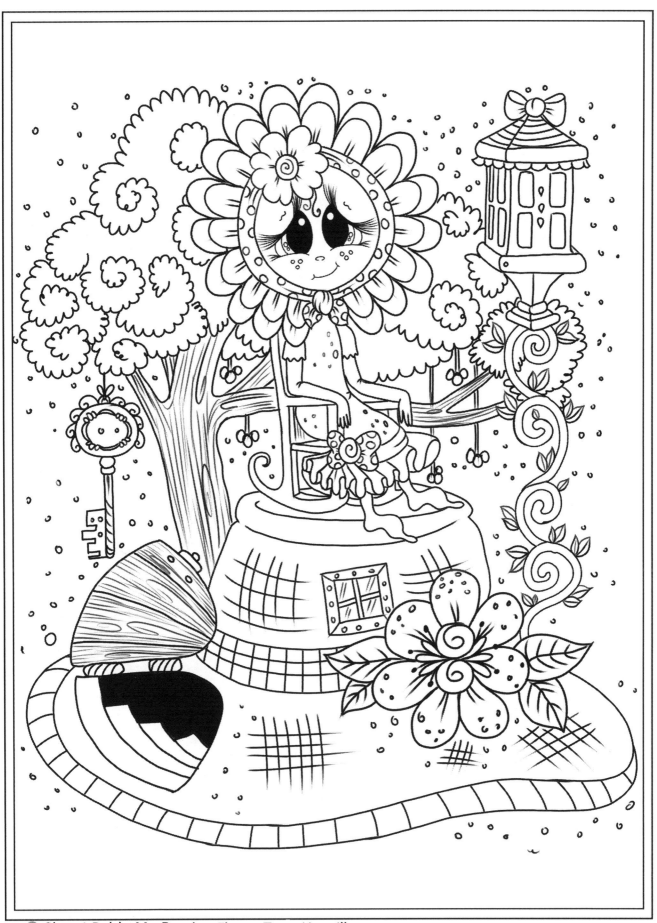

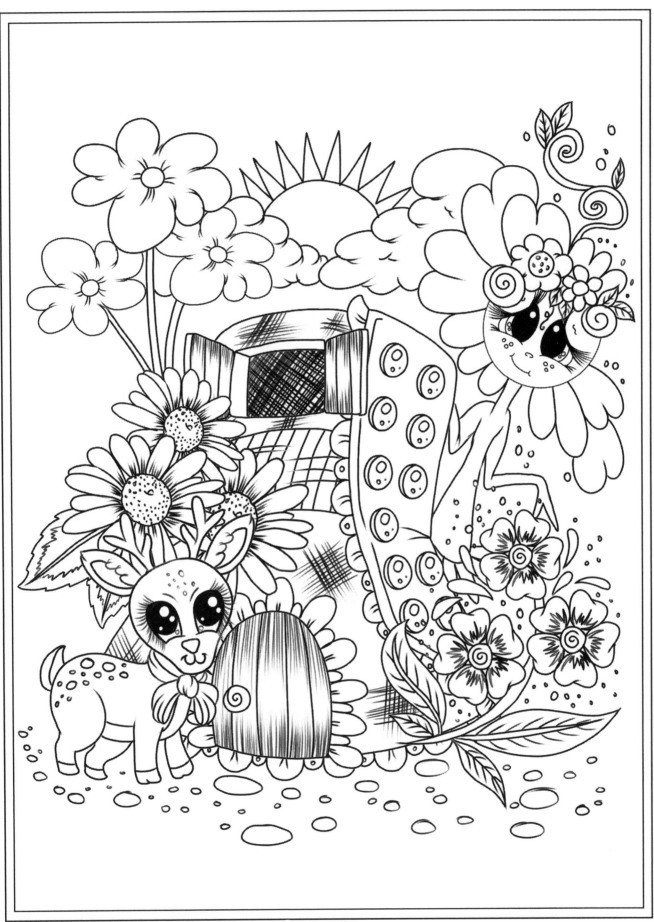

© Sherri Baldy My-Besties Flower Town Hat-ville

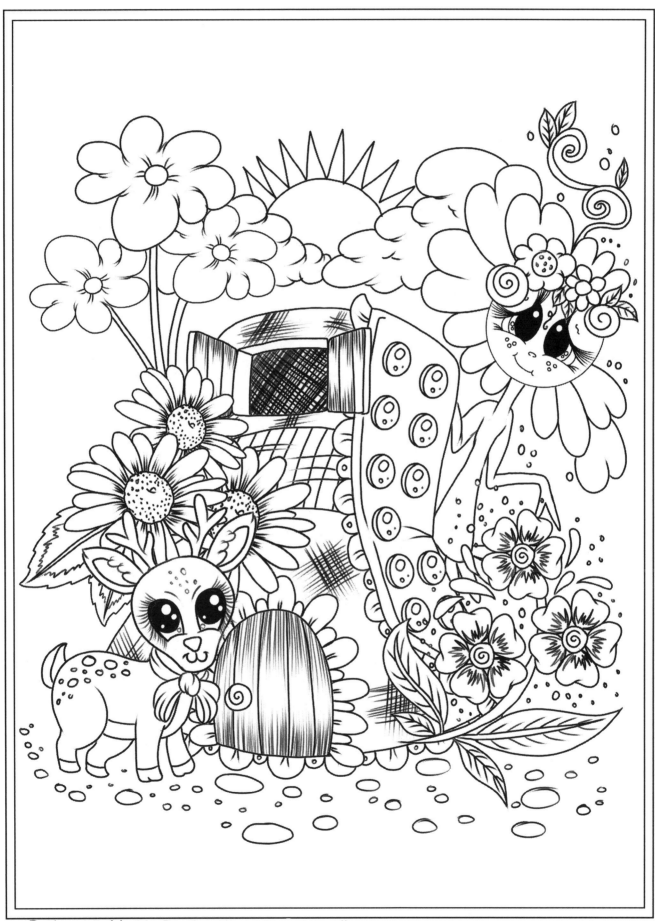

© Sherri Baldy My-Besties Flower Town Hat-ville

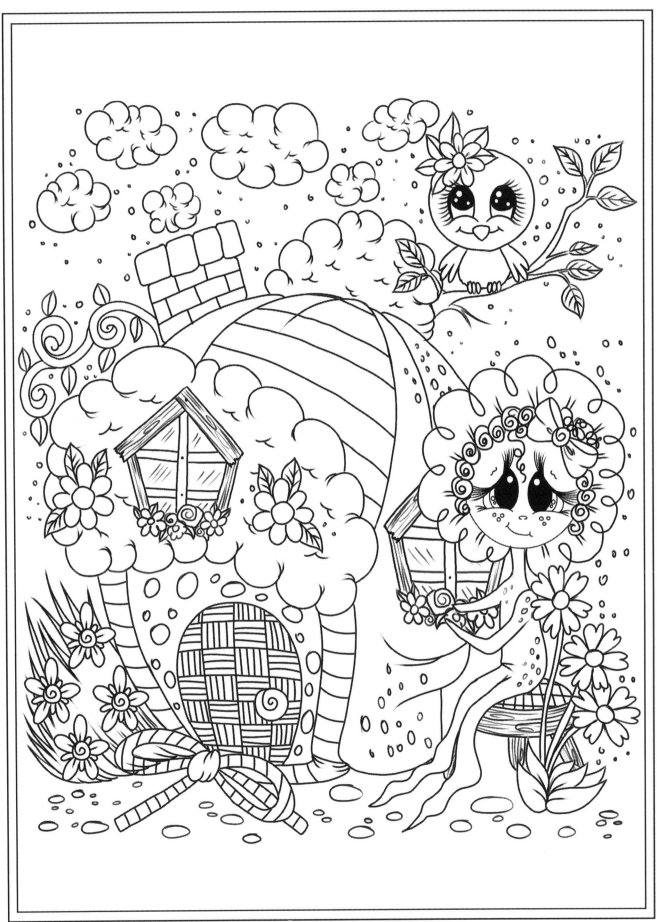

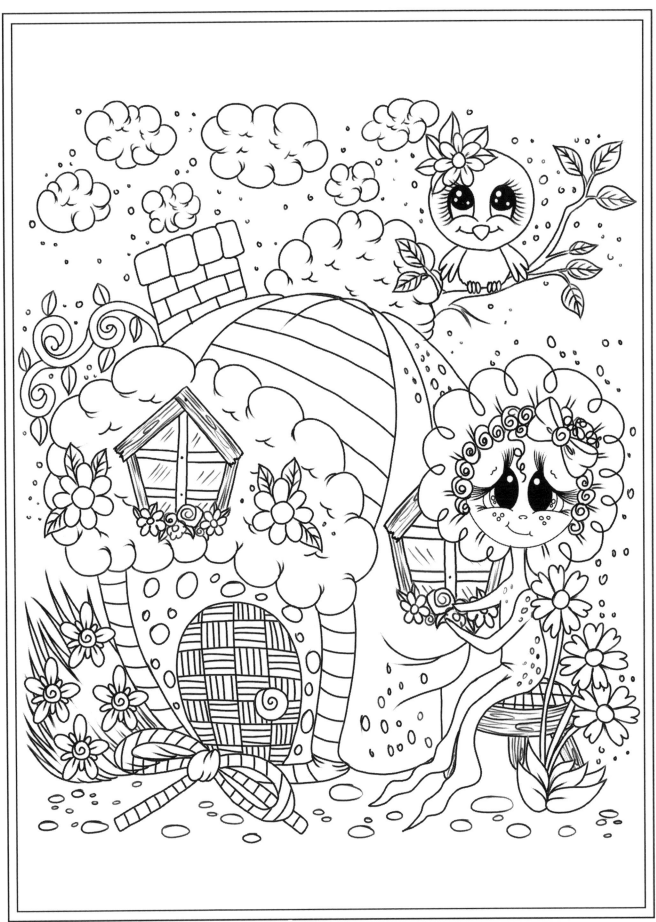

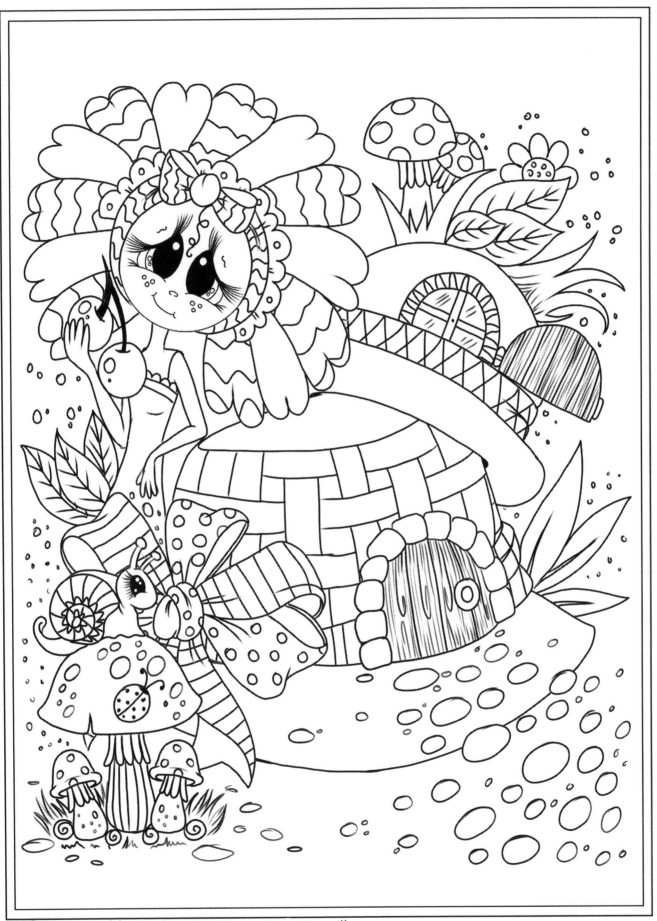

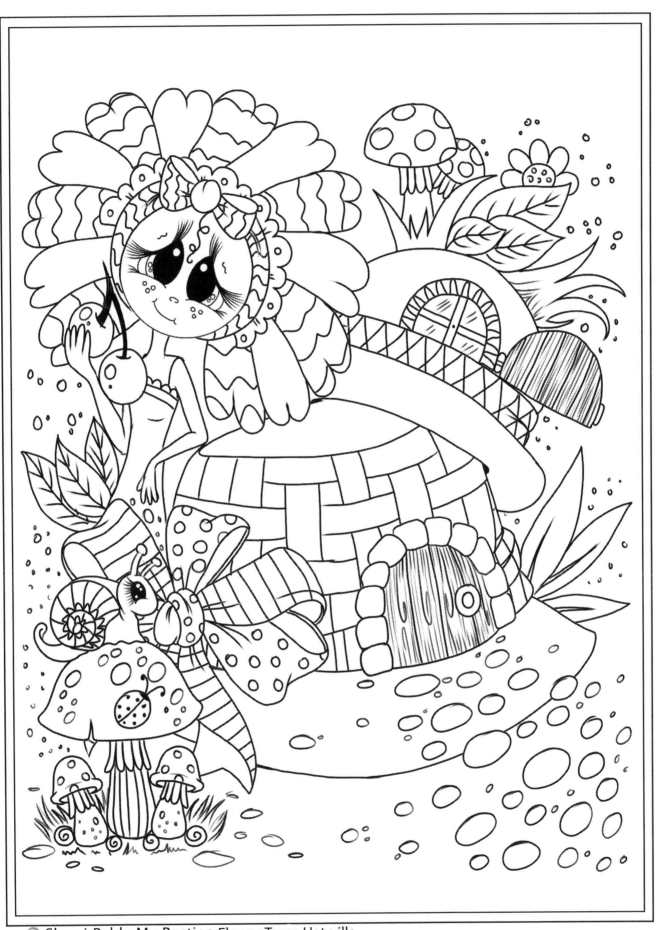

© Sherri Baldy My-Besties Flower Town Hat-ville

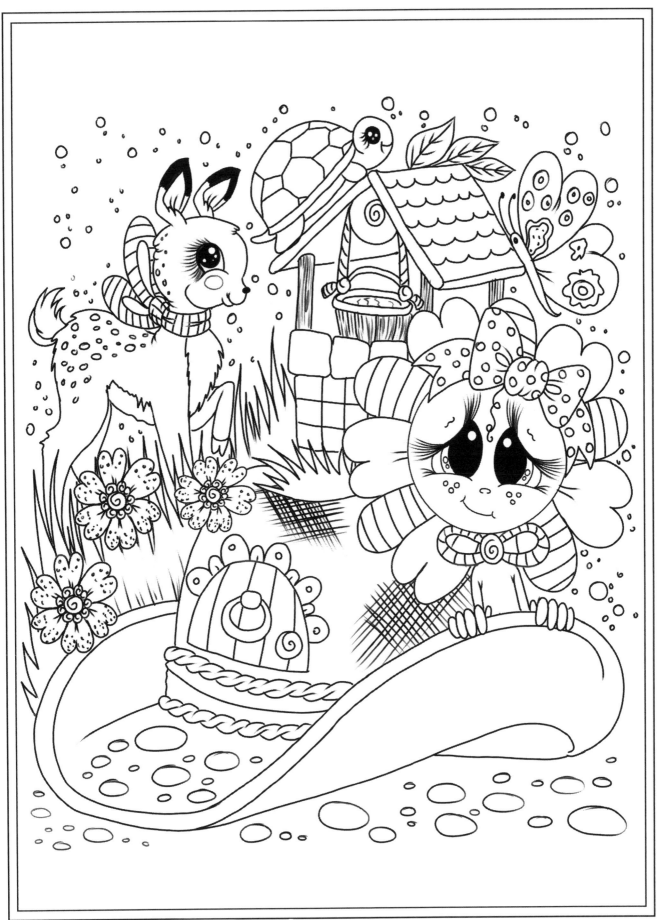

© Sherri Baldy My-Besties Flower Town Hat-ville

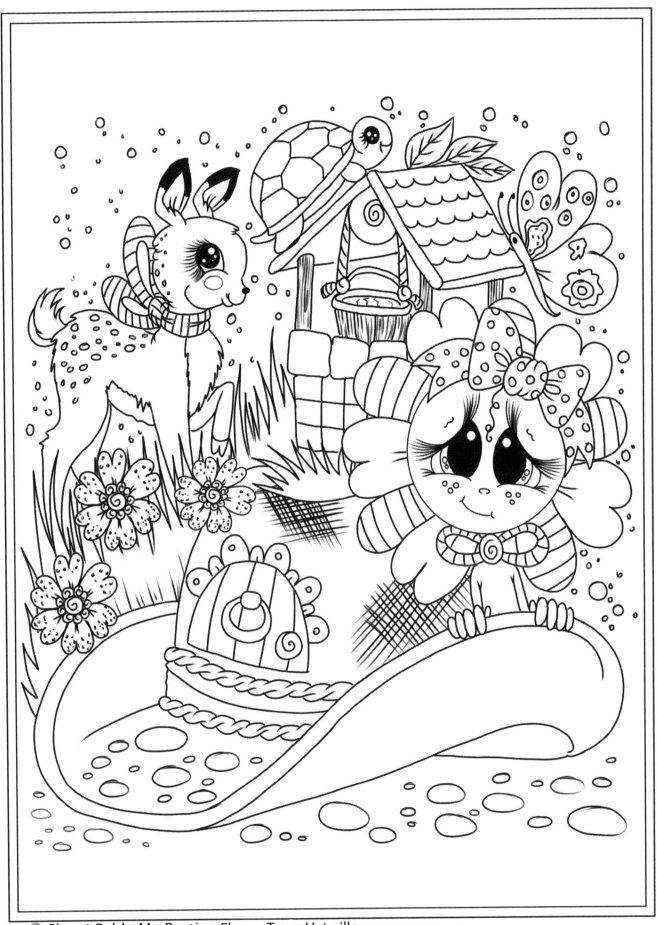

© Sherri Baldy My-Besties Flower Town Hat-ville

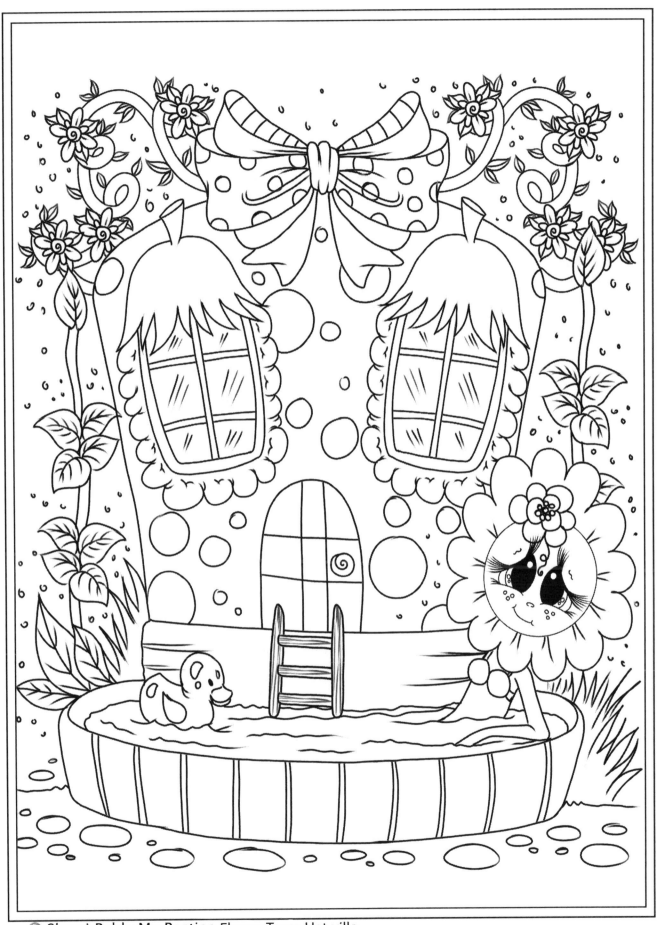

© Sherri Baldy My-Besties Flower Town Hat-ville

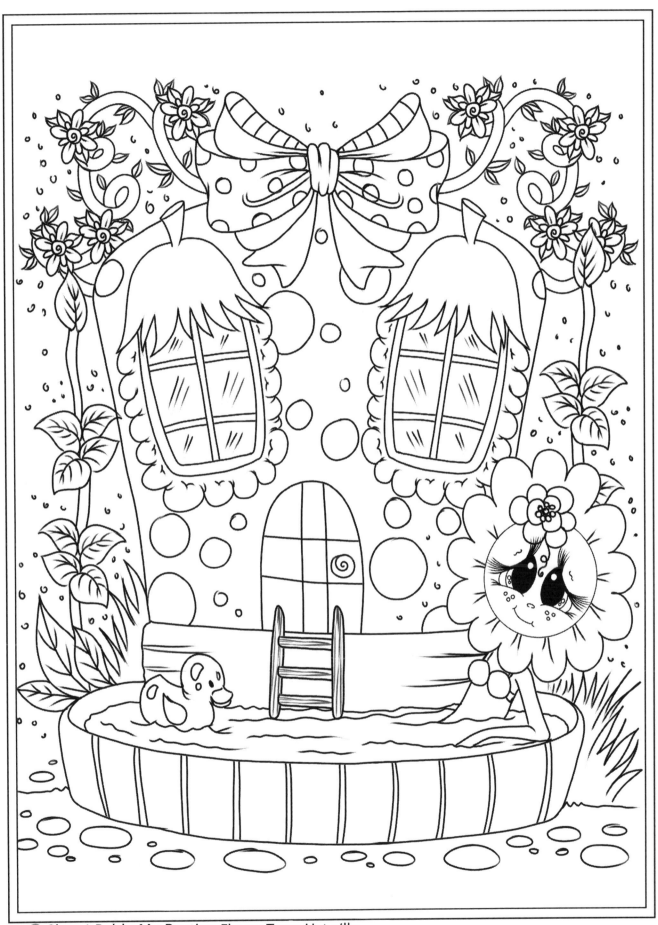

Coloring Books by Sherri Baldy

1. Gnome-Ville
2. Halloween Adorable Besties
3. Have a little Faith Besties
4. Fall Days
5. Flower Petal Pots
6. Fluffy's 1
7. Fluffy's 2
8. You drive me Batty
9. Spookylicious
10. Pinkles the Pink frog & Friends
11. I love Coffee
12. Adorable Blooms & Spring Things
13. My Besties Monsters Ever mini monsters
14. Lil Monsters 2
15. Alphabet Besties
16. Back to School
17. Christmas Cottage
18. Trick or Treat
19. Coloring Book Calendar & Birthstone Besties
20. Fairy Princess
21. Lil Rascals
22. Little Dimples
23. Little Rosie's Christmas
24. Flirty Fluffies
25. Magical Creatures & Enchanted PLaces
26. Magical Winter
27. Messy Bessy Jessy
28. Moon & Stars
29. Night before Christmas
30. Besties of Oz
31. Pets
32. Santa's Little Helpers
33. Some Bunny Loves you
34. Sweet heart
35. The magic of winter
36. Warm Christmas Nights
37. Birthday Coloring Book

Coloring Books by Sherri Baldy

38. Bloomin Besties
39. Boys Rule
40. Busy Bees & Butterflies
41. Cat Lovers
42. Cat Lovers (Cat Ladies)
43. Chibi
44. Ella Bella Buttons and Bows
45. Enchanted Unicorns
46. Fairy Time
47. Giggle Box Girls
48. Here's My Heart
49. Hoppy Spring Qt's
50. Hot Cocoa
51. Making Faces
52. Pat & The Bird Ladies
53. Steampunk
54. Sweet Treats
55. Tea Time
56. Tiny & her supersaurus & Knobby knee Besties
57. Halloween Coloring Book Boo
58. Winter Wonderland Filled with Love
59. Under the sea mermaids
60. Winter Snowmen
61. Zen Art
62. Zodiac and Star Gazers
63. Slinky Fashionista
64. Steampunk Sweethearts
65. Alice and the looking glass
66. Sweet Geeks
67. Twinkle Toe Trolls
68. Vintage Mermaids
69. Puppy Love
70. Flowertown (Feb 2019)
71. Flowertown Home is where the heart is (Feb 2019)
72. Magical Nutcracker (Dec 2018)
73. The Joys of Winter (Dec 2018)
74. Fantastical Winter (Nov 2018)
75. Fan Club Favorites 2018 (Nov 2018)

Coloring Books by Sherri Baldy

Welcome to My Besties World!
Sherri invites you to come join in her SUPER Friendly and FUN Crafting community!
We always look forward to seeing ALL the Sherri Baldy My-Besties Creations by our coloring, crafter friends from all around the world and We LOVE meeting and making NEW Friends!
Come PARTY with us every few weeks at our FB FUN NEW Releases where we have Loads of Giveaways, Name Games going on and Freebies!!!
We share tips, tricks and techniques. Join in on the FUN coloring & crafting group here:
https://www.facebook.com/groups/mybestiesdesigns/
Our crafty group is a safe fun place for you to post all your My Bestie Colorings, Creations, Photos, Blog Posts, and More..... anything featuring our My Besties Images, Stamps and Sherri Baldy Crafting Products are welcome!
We have MANY Shops for you to enjoy featuring Sherri Baldy My Bestie Craft Products!
Our My Bestie Shops:
www.MyBestiesShop.com
www.My-Besties.com
www.Scrapbookstampsociety.com

Our Etys Shop:
https://www.etsy.com/shop/SherriBaldy?ref=hdr_shop_menu

Join our Blog Challenges:

Our Sherri Baldy Blog:http://sherribaldy.blogspot.com/

Sherri Baldy

Color With Sherri & The Besties!

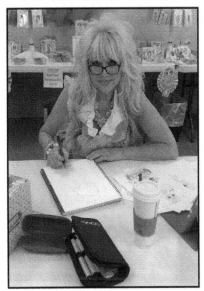
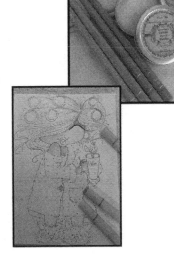

Made in the USA
Lexington, KY
11 July 2019